Original title:
Echoes of Us

Copyright © 2024 Swan Charm
All rights reserved.

Author: Olivia Orav
ISBN HARDBACK: 978-9916-79-173-8
ISBN PAPERBACK: 978-9916-79-174-5
ISBN EBOOK: 978-9916-79-175-2

# Within the Holy Circle

In silence we gather, hearts intertwined,
A circle of light where souls are aligned.
Together we stand, in faith we believe,
In whispers of grace, we take and receive.

Hand in hand, we share sacred breath,
In moments of stillness, we conquer our death.
With spirits in harmony, we lift up our song,
In this holy circle, to Him we belong.

Each prayer like a blossom, reaching the skies,
With hope as our anchor, our spirits arise.
From the depths of our hearts, we cast out the doubt,
Within the divine love, our fears are cast out.

The flames of the candles dance bright in the night,
Illuminating paths with their mystical light.
In the warmth of His presence, our burdens erase,
For in this holy gathering, we find our true place.

Renewed by the spirit, we strive for the peace,
In trust, we surrender, all struggles shall cease.
With whispers of wisdom, our souls are made whole,
Within the holy circle, we meet and console.

## **Mirrored in Eternity**

In stillness we breathe, heaven's embrace,
Reflecting the light, a sacred grace.
Within our hearts, a whisper divine,
Eternity's echo, in silence we shine.

Each moment a gift, a thread of the past,
Binding our souls, forever steadfast.
In the dance of the stars, our spirits unite,
Mirrored in love, we find our true sight.

## Abiding in Remembrance

In the quiet, we gather, in prayer we stand,
Remembering those, who walked 'neath this land.
Their voices still linger, like soft-spoken dreams,
Guiding our hearts, or so it would seem.

With every soft glimmer, their wisdom we seek,
In times of stillness, when shadows grow weak.
Abiding in love, our souls intertwine,
In remembrance we flourish, eternally shine.

## **Divine Threads Woven**

Threads of existence, delicate and bright,
Woven by hands, unseen in the night.
Each life a tapestry, rich with the hue,
Of love and of loss, of joy and of rue.

In the fabric of time, our stories align,
A sacred design, in the realm of the divine.
Together we rise, together we fall,
In the weft of the cosmos, we answer the call.

## The Timeless Connection

In the dawn's first light, we find our way,
A timeless connection, come what may.
In the stillness of night, our spirits take flight,
Bound by a promise, in love's endless light.

Through valleys and peaks, our journeys unfold,
In whispers of truth, ancient and bold.
The threads of our faith, like stars in the sky,
Illuminate paths, as we learn to fly.

## **Celestial Murmurs**

In the quiet morn we raise,
Voices lifted high in praise.
Stars alight, a guiding beam,
Whispers soft, a sacred dream.

Heaven's echoes fill the air,
Grace bestowed, a gentle care.
Each heart beats in time with love,
Unified, we rise above.

Mountains stand, bathed in light,
Creation sings in pure delight.
By the stream, where blessings flow,
Peace surrounds, and spirits glow.

In the shadows, hope ignites,
Faith ignited through long nights.
Together we shall tread this path,
Finding joy in sacred math.

Let us walk with humble grace,
Side by side in this embrace.
Through celestial murmurs, we find,
The whispers of a love divine.

## The Spirit's Resonance

Breathe in deep the morning air,
Feel the pulse of love laid bare.
In stillness, our spirits rise,
Reflecting light from endless skies.

Voices echo through the trees,
Nature sings, a gentle breeze.
In every leaf, a story told,
Of ancient truths and faiths bold.

Hearts entwined, we dance in prayer,
Finding strength in love's soft glare.
In unity our souls align,
Resonating through the divine.

Journey forth, hand in hand,
Faithful hearts across the land.
With each step, let kindness flow,
Together strong, we'll help each grow.

In the silence, hear the call,
The spirit's voice, it binds us all.
As one we rise, through light we see,
Together found, forever free.

## Hymns of Our Togetherness

Gathered here, in sacred space,
Each soul shines with holy grace.
In the chorus, voices merge,
Harmony begins to surge.

Through trials, we stand as one,
In the night, we seek the sun.
With our hands, we lift each heart,
In this unity, we start.

Songs of hope, they fill the air,
In every verse, a loving care.
Let our spirits intertwine,
Creating bonds, a holy line.

Every smile, a shared delight,
In the darkness, we find light.
Through the storms that test our ground,
In our love, the strength is found.

Hymns arise, sweet melodies,
Celebrating life's mysteries.
In togetherness, we ascend,
A sacred journey without end.

## Ethereal Footprints

On this earth, we walk with grace,
Every step a sacred place.
In the cosmos, ancient ties,
In our hearts, the wisdom lies.

Follow paths of light that shine,
In the stillness, love's design.
Guided by a gentle hand,
Making footprints in the sand.

Through the trials, we find our way,
In the night, we seek the day.
Together, in the light we blend,
Ethereal footprints without end.

With each breath, a prayer we send,
Trusting that our hearts will mend.
In the whispers of the breeze,
Feel the calm that put us at ease.

So let us walk with heads held high,
With love's promise, we can fly.
In the dance of life, we see,
Ethereal prints in unity.

## The Faithful Return

In the dusk of twilight's glow,
Hearts return, like rivers flow.
With hands raised up to the skies,
Voices lift, as silence dies.

Through valleys deep, where shadows play,
Faithful souls find their way.
Guided by a holy light,
They seek the truth within the night.

Mountains high and oceans wide,
On this journey, they abide.
Every step, a prayer confides,
In the arms of love, they bide.

With every tear, a lesson learned,
Through every scar, a heart discerned.
Together, they stand, hand in hand,
The faithful return to holy land.

## Whispers of the Divine

In the stillness of the morn,
Voices sweetly, gently borne.
Whispers soft like gentle breeze,
Echo through the swaying trees.

From the depths of silent prayer,
Messages float rich in air.
Hearts attune to sacred calls,
Where the spirit ever sprawls.

In each moment, grace bestowed,
Pathways clear, and burdens shed.
In the dusk, the stars ignite,
Guiding souls through endless night.

Trust the whispers, let them in,
A tapestry where hope begins.
In the quiet, truth will shine,
Leading us to the divine.

## **Remnants of Faith**

In the ashes of despair,
Hope remains, vibrant and rare.
Through storms that rage and skies of grey,
Faith flickers, lighting the way.

Memories wrapped in sacred grace,
Hold the remnants in their place.
Every prayer, a seed so small,
Yet, they rise above the fall.

In the ruins, blessings bloom,
From the darkness, dispelling gloom.
They whisper truths of love and care,
Binding hearts with threads so rare.

In the depths of every soul,
Remnants of faith make us whole.
With courage fierce, we shall ignite,
A testament of love and light.

## Shadows of our Spirits

In the silence of the night,
Shadows dance in silver light.
Hidden truths, they start to show,
Guiding spirits as they flow.

In the corners of the mind,
Wonders wait for hearts aligned.
Echoes of what used to be,
Whispers soft, eternally.

Through the trials, shadows wane,
In the struggle, still remain.
Yet through every darkened plight,
Shadows lead us toward the light.

Embrace the shadows, hold them near,
For they teach us to revere.
In their presence, truths impart,
Shadows shape the faithful heart.

# Tracing the Celestial Path

In the quiet of the night, stars gleam,
Guiding souls with a radiant beam.
Through the shadows, a whisper calls,
Seeking grace in the heavenly halls.

Footsteps light on the sacred ground,
With every prayer, a heartbeat found.
From the depths, to the sky so vast,
We trace the path, of ages past.

Guided by the light above,
Wings of hope, and boundless love.
In every moment, the truth reveals,
The harmony that the spirit feels.

Through trials faced, we rise and stand,
With faith igniting, hand in hand.
The universe sings in unity,
Embracing all in divinity.

With each dawn, a new design,
A tapestry of life divine.
The echoes sing of what will be,
Tracing the path to eternity.

## Divine Murmurs Among Us

In every heart resides a flame,
A whisper soft, yet never tame.
Echoes of love, pure and bright,
Divine murmurs in the night.

Through the silence, wisdom flows,
Guiding us where the spirit grows.
In the laughter, and in the tears,
We find the strength to face our fears.

The wind carries a sacred song,
A melody where all belong.
In the rustle of leaves, we hear,
The voice of grace ever near.

Hand in hand, we walk this earth,
Finding beauty in our worth.
In the moments shared, we see,
A dance of souls in harmony.

With every breath, a prayer ascends,
In the heart's deep, love transcends.
The divine whispers its gentle lore,
Binding us forevermore.

## The Unity of Spirit

In the stillness, a soft embrace,
We seek the light, we seek the grace.
Together, as one, we rise in prayer,
Connecting hearts in the sacred air.

Each step taken in faith's glow,
A journey where our spirits flow.
With every smile, and every tear,
We draw the divine ever near.

Amidst the chaos, find the peace,
In unity, our doubts release.
As rivers merge and become the sea,
We find our strength in harmony.

Let the spirit guide our way,
Illuminating each new day.
In the whispers of the trees,
We hear the call of love's sweet breeze.

In joyful hearts, the truth we sing,
With open arms, the heavens bring.
A chorus of souls, forever free,
In divine love's unity.

## Tides of the Sacred Sea

Waves roll in with a solemn grace,
Echoing tales of the human race.
Tides of change, a sacred flow,
Carrying lessons for hearts to know.

Upon the shore, we make our mark,
In the dance of light, we ignite a spark.
With every crash, a story told,
Of faith, of love, and courage bold.

The ocean whispers secrets deep,
In its embrace, our worries sleep.
In the ebb and flow, we find our peace,
A tranquil heart that will not cease.

As the sun dips low in twilight's hue,
We gather strength, to start anew.
Embracing the tides, we rise and fall,
In the sacred sea, we hear the call.

In the currents, a spirit free,
Guiding us through life's mystery.
With every wave that greets the shore,
We stand united, forevermore.

## Divine Reflections

In silence, I seek Your grace,
Your love a gentle embrace.
Each whisper leads my heart,
A journey where I will not part.

In shadows, Your light breaks through,
Guiding me in all I pursue.
A mirror of truth I find,
In the depths of my humble mind.

Your essence like a fragrant bloom,
In every corner, dispelling the gloom.
I ponder the vast and divine,
In the stillness, Your spirit shines.

From mountains high to valleys low,
Your presence, a river's flow.
In each heartbeat, I feel the call,
To rise up, surrender, and fall.

So here I stand, heart open wide,
With faith as my ever-present guide.
In reflections, I see Your face,
In Your arms, I find my place.

## Hallowed Murmurs

O sacred whispers fill the night,
Carried on the wings of light.
In gentle cadence, voices blend,
Calling forth the timeless friend.

Your name, a melody so pure,
In my spirit, a ceaseless cure.
With each prayer, a petal falls,
Soft blessings within hallowed halls.

Lifted high on wings of hope,
Through trials, I learn to cope.
Each murmur, a promise to hold,
In the warmth, Your love unfolds.

The world spins on, yet I remain,
In solitude, I find no pain.
For in the quiet, there's a space,
Where hallowed murmurs bless my grace.

With humble heart, I walk this path,
In Your wisdom, I find my math.
Each step a prayer, each breath a hymn,
Eternally grateful, though dim.

## Messages in the Mist

In morning's dew, a mystery unfolds,
Messages of love, divine stories told.
Veils of fog hide what's ahead,
Yet trust is born where angels tread.

Soft whispers brush against my ear,
Guiding me through shadows of fear.
Each drop a note in a sacred song,
A reminder that I truly belong.

As twilight descends and dreams arise,
I seek the truth beyond the skies.
In every heart, a sacred plea,
For clarity in the great mystery.

Through the haze, Your message shines bright,
A beacon in the enveloping night.
In the mist, I find my way,
With faith as my banner each day.

The silence holds more than it seems,
A tapestry woven with hopes and dreams.
So let me walk where the spirits guide,
In the mist, my soul abides.

## The Law of Belonging

In the heart of creation, I find,
A bond that weaves through all mankind.
The law of love, ever strong,
In each spirit, we all belong.

Through trials faced, we learn to see,
The threads that tie you and me.
In laughter shared, in tears combined,
The beauty of being intertwined.

In every doubt, a truth remains,
No soul is lost; no love in vain.
Hand in hand, the journey flows,
A sacred path where compassion grows.

As stars unite in the canvas of night,
So too do we, with hearts alight.
In unity's grace, we rise and sing,
With harmony born from the offering.

For the law of belonging, forever is,
A divine dance in the cosmic bliss.
Each life a note in the symphony's song,
Together we flourish, together we're strong.

## Verses of the Infinite

In whispers soft, the heavens speak,
Echoes of love, in silence peak.
Stars align, a guiding light,
In the heart of the endless night.

Faithful souls in dance entwined,
In the embrace of the divine.
Graces bestowed from realms above,
All creation sings of love.

Transcend the bounds of time and space,
In every trial, find His grace.
With every breath, a sacred prayer,
Life's burdens lifted, none to bear.

Journeys vast, yet one we stand,
Together in His mighty hand.
In every tear, a shining spark,
Illuminating the path through dark.

With open hearts, we seek the throne,
In trials faced, we're never alone.
For in the depths, our spirits rise,
In verses of the infinite skies.

## **Memories Beneath the Sacred Veil**

Beneath the veil where whispers dwell,
Memories linger, tales to tell.
In sacred shadows, grace does flow,
Love's eternal, gentle glow.

Fleeting moments, caught in time,
Hearts entwined, in rhythm, rhyme.
Every heartbeat sings a song,
A melody where we belong.

In the silence, wisdom speaks,
Nurtured hopes, and quiet seeks.
Guarded dreams, in faith we tread,
In paths of light where angels led.

Embrace the dawn, let shadows fade,
A tapestry of love is laid.
In every prayer, a seed is sown,
In sacred soil, our faith has grown.

Together we rise, hand in hand,
Beneath the veil, our spirits stand.
With every breath, a life renewed,
In memories sweet, our souls imbued.

## Seraphic Songs of Memory

In skies of blue, the seraphs sing,
Notes of joy to hearts they bring.
With every chord, the heavens sway,
In harmony, we find our way.

Echoes of love in the breeze,
Soft reminders, our hearts appease.
In sacred songs, our past unveiled,
Where hope and faith have never failed.

Tales of journeys, trials faced,
With every step, His love embraced.
In memories held, we find our might,
Guided by the eternal light.

Lessons learned from days of yore,
In every tear, a chance to soar.
The seraphs' song, a radiant glow,
In every heart, let gratitude flow.

Awake our spirits, lift them high,
In seraphic songs, we touch the sky.
Together we'll carry love's refrain,
In memories sweet, we rise again.

## Celestial Embrace

In the quiet of the night, we dream,
Under stars that softly gleam.
In celestial whispers, hearts align,
Embraced by love, forever mine.

Voices echo in the stillness bright,
Guiding us through the endless night.
In every challenge, hope ignites,
With faith as our eternal light.

Angels watch from realms above,
Wrapping us in gentle love.
In moments shared, no fear remains,
In celestial joy, our spirit gains.

Together we dance in sacred space,
Experiencing heaven's grace.
With open arms, let burdens cease,
In every heartbeat, find our peace.

With every sunrise, promise anew,
In celestial embrace, we are true.
A journey blessed, hand in hand,
Bound by love, forever we stand.

## The Light within Shadows

In the darkness, Your grace shines,
Guiding souls with whispered signs.
Through valleys deep, and trials wide,
Your love, O Lord, will be our guide.

When doubts arise and hearts feel cold,
Your warmth, a promise, truth behold.
In every shadow, there's a spark,
Your light ignites the paths we embark.

With faith, we rise from ash and dust,
In every struggle, in You we trust.
A beacon bright, our souls' delight,
Leading us home from darkest night.

In quiet moments, we find our peace,
Your presence brings our fears to cease.
Among the chaos, Your whispers clear,
In every heart, we hold You near.

O ever-present, ever kind,
In shadows deep, Your love we find.
Forever through us, let it flow,
The light within, forever glow.

## Missives from the Depths

From the depths of sorrow, cries arise,
Silent prayers carried to the skies.
In darkest waters, hope is sown,
Through every struggle, we are not alone.

Each tear a missive, each sigh a song,
In the valley of shadows, we still belong.
Your mercy blankets our weary souls,
In aching hearts, Your comfort rolls.

In whispered winds, our fears collide,
But in Your love, our doubts subside.
To the depths we call, with voices clear,
O Lord, in You, our hearts draw near.

We rise on wings, like eagles bold,
In faith unyielding, our spirits hold.
The currents may pull, but we will stand,
With every heartbeat, held in Your hand.

In the depths of night, we find the dawn,
With every missive, a spirit reborn.
For in our darkest, You are the light,
Guiding us through, with love infinite.

## Ancestral Chants

Through ages past, the echoes flow,
In ancestral chants, the wisdom grows.
Each voice a thread, in unity spun,
Binding our hearts until we are one.

Oh, sacred songs of those long gone,
In every verse, their spirits drawn.
Through trials faced, and battles fought,
In every prayer, their lessons taught.

The fire burns bright in the gathering night,
Illuminating paths with ancient light.
With every heartbeat, we hum their themes,
In the fabric of life, we weave their dreams.

As we gather, let our voices rise,
In harmony under vast, open skies.
For in remembrance, we seek the way,
Leading us gently to brighter days.

These chants of old, hold truth divine,
Connecting generations, sacred line.
Through every song, we honor their gift,
Ancestral whispers, our spirits lift.

## **Soulful Resonance**

In the stillness, our souls entwine,
A celestial dance, pure and divine.
Every heartbeat a note, every breath a prayer,
In the sacred union, You are there.

Through trials and triumphs, we resonate,
Your love, a melody, we celebrate.
In each moment, Your grace we feel,
With soulful cadence, our hearts heal.

Each note a story, each sigh a plea,
A symphony of life, eternally free.
From mountain tops to valleys deep,
In the rhythm of faith, our spirits leap.

As harmonies rise in the evening glow,
We find our purpose, in love we sow.
Your voice, a whisper, guides our way,
In every struggle, You light the day.

Together we journey, hand in hand,
In soulful resonance, forever we stand.
Through every trial, Your presence near,
Our hearts sing out, in joy sincere.

## **Glimpses of the Eternal**

In the silence of dawn's gentle grace,
We seek the light of a holy face.
Moments captured, time stands still,
As hearts awaken to divine will.

Whispers carried on the morning breeze,
Touching souls with celestial ease.
A reflection of love, pure and bright,
Guiding us through the shadowy night.

Every star a promise, shining clear,
Reminders of blessings ever near.
In peace we gather, in faith we rise,
Embracing the truth that never dies.

With hands uplifted, we share our dreams,
In unity, where grace redeems.
Each heartbeat echoes the sacred song,
In the spaces where we all belong.

So let us journey, with spirits bold,
Finding warmth in the stories told.
For in the glimpses of the eternal light,
We discover heaven within our sight.

## Spheres of the Sanctified

In realms of grace, where angels dwell,
Echoes of faith in a sacred swell.
Hearts entwined in celestial dance,
Together we rise, in holy romance.

Each prayer a star, brightening the night,
Illuminating paths with hope's sweet light.
Spheres of the sanctified, ever near,
Whispering love in each silent tear.

Harmony flows like a river's song,
Binding us gently, where we belong.
Together we wander through valleys wide,
With spirit as compass, and God as our guide.

In moments of doubt, we find our strength,
As faith surrounds us in measured length.
Each breath a testament, a sacred vow,
To seek the divine in the here and now.

So let us stand, hand in hand we pray,
Join hearts and voices, come what may.
For in the spheres where sanctified roam,
We find our refuge, we find our home.

# **The Whispering Light**

Softly it calls, the whispering light,
Guiding the weary through darkest night.
In shadows that linger, fear takes flight,
As hope unfolds in the dawning sight.

A flicker of faith, a glimpse of grace,
Filling our hearts in this sacred space.
In troubled times, it leads the way,
And comforts our souls as we humbly pray.

Through valleys low and mountains high,
The light, it beckons, drawing nigh.
Each step a prayer, each sigh a song,
In the realm of light, we all belong.

Embrace the warmth of the Savior's love,
As it shines down from the heavens above.
In unity, we gather, hand in hand,
A tapestry woven by the divine plan.

Now let the whispering light ignite,
The hearts of the faithful, both day and night.
For in the glow, we find our way,
Together in purpose, we rise and pray.

## **Petals of Our Prayers**

Each morning blooms with petals bright,
As we offer up our prayers in light.
With hands like flowers, reaching high,
We trust the heavens, as dreams comply.

The garden of hope flourishes wide,
In every tear, the will to abide.
Petals of faith, cast gently here,
Each fragrant whisper, divine and clear.

In gratitude's embrace, we lift our voice,
Finding solace in the heart's choice.
With every petal, a promise made,
In love's embrace, no fear will wade.

Together we stand, in joy and strife,
Nurturing the bonds that expand our life.
As petals fall, they weave a tale,
Of the sacred journey where love prevails.

So let our prayers be gardens of grace,
Abundant blessings in every place.
Through fields of faith, may our spirits soar,
With petals of prayer forevermore.

**Aligning With the Divine**

In stillness, we seek the sacred light,
A whisper guiding through the night.
Our souls unveil the truth we bind,
In the quiet, we trust, aligned with the divine.

Heaven's echo calls us near,
With every heartbeat, we sense the clear.
In gentle waves, the spirit flows,
Through love's embrace, our essence grows.

Through trials faced, we find our way,
In faith and grace, we shall not sway.
On golden paths, our hopes arise,
United under ever-watchful skies.

With open hearts, we learn to share,
The light within, a sacred prayer.
Each moment crafted, each breath profound,
In whispered promises, our lives are found.

When shadows loom and doubts descend,
In trust, we fold, in love, we mend.
For in the darkness, shines the dawn,
With every step, we carry on.

## **The Lightning of Belonging**

In thunder's roar, connections spark,
A holy bond igniting the dark.
Electric heartbeats resonate,
In unity, we cultivate our fate.

The sky illuminates our shared plight,
In storms, we find our sacred might.
Through trials fierce, we learn to grow,
In sacred circles, love will flow.

With every flash, the truth revealed,
In moments rare, our wounds are healed.
The pulse of life, a vibrant force,
Together journey, we find our course.

The brush of fate we cannot ignore,
In paths entwined, we seek for more.
This lightning strikes our very core,
In grace we find what we adore.

A tapestry of souls so bright,
In each embrace, we claim the light.
In wildest storms, we stand as one,
Through chaos, our belonging's spun.

## Myriad of Sacred Threads

In woven tales of joy and tears,
A tapestry of love appears.
Each sacred thread, a story spun,
In every heart, the colors run.

Through ancient hands, the loom is cast,
In holy moments, time stands fast.
Connecting souls in vibrant hue,
In unity, we create anew.

A network strong, no strand left bare,
Every breath, a whispered prayer.
In woven paths, our shadows blend,
Together in grace, we shall transcend.

In gentle hands, we pull the seams,
With every knot, we weave our dreams.
A myriad of hearts, one grand design,
In love's embrace, we're truly divine.

As nights unfold, the stars align,
In every heart, the sacred shrine.
We celebrate the ties that bind,
In this great weave, our souls enshrined.

## **The Pawns of Providence**

In holy play, we take our stand,
Pawns of fate, in His great hand.
Each move we make, a dance divine,
In providence, our paths entwine.

With every choice, a chance to grow,
In trust, we learn, in faith, we sow.
The game unfolds, each sacrifice,
In sacred lessons, there lies the price.

Through trials steep, in sorrow's grip,
Each challenge faced, we learn to slip.
For in the struggle, wisdom's gained,
In losses felt, abundance reigns.

As humble pawns, we play our parts,
In every move, we give our hearts.
Destiny weaves its wondrous thread,
In silent whispers, we're gently led.

In every heartbeat, guidance flows,
In every trial, the spirit grows.
With grace upon this sacred board,
As pawns, we rise, embraced by the Lord.

## The Intertwining of Souls

In the silence where spirits meet,
Hearts embrace in sacred light.
Threads of love, gentle and sweet,
Binding us through day and night.

Each moment a prayer we share,
Whispers carried on the breeze.
In your gaze, I find my care,
Together, we are at ease.

Through trials, our faith does grow,
Like the roots of ancient trees.
In the shadows, love will glow,
Carving paths to inner peace.

In the dance of life we sway,
Hand in hand, we walk as one.
Underneath the stars, we pray,
Trusting journeys yet begun.

From the depths to endless heights,
Souls entwined, no bond can break.
In the stillness, love ignites,
A flame only we can make.

## Fragments of the Common Heart

Each soul a piece, a vibrant hue,
Together forming a grand whole.
In our struggles, we find the true,
Unity woven deep in soul.

Hands outstretched, we lift the weak,
Compassion flows like rivers wide.
In our hearts, the love we seek,
Guiding us where hope resides.

In the laughter, in the tears,
Echoes of a shared refrain.
Through the ages, through the years,
Common bonds endure the pain.

From the ashes, we arise,
Together strong, we forge ahead.
With open hearts and joyful cries,
We illuminate where hope is spread.

Fragments joined, a radiant light,
Together, we transcend the dark.
In our union, we find the might,
For love ignites the brightest spark.

## Celestial Whispers

In the stillness of the night,
Stars above sing softly clear.
With each glimmer, pure delight,
Heaven's breath draws our hearts near.

In the whispers of the breeze,
Secrets carried from afar.
Nature's voice, it brings us peace,
Guiding us to where we are.

Every raindrop, every sigh,
Messages from realms divine.
Through the chaos, we can fly,
Transcending limits by design.

On the wings of faith, we soar,
Embracing all that is and will.
In the quiet, we explore,
Celestial realms that thrill.

United in this sacred space,
Listening to the cosmic call.
In our hearts, we find our place,
In the silence, we are all.

## **Illuminated Paths**

In the darkness, shadows play,
Yet we seek the guiding light.
With each step, we find the way,
Trusting love to hold us tight.

Through the valleys and the streams,
Hopes are shining like the sun.
Every prayer, a sacred beam,
Lighting paths for everyone.

In the journey, hand in hand,
No one walks this road alone.
Together, we will make our stand,
Finding strength in every stone.

With our spirits intertwined,
We embrace the endless fight.
In our hearts, the truth defined,
Illuminated by love's light.

May our footsteps leave a trace,
An echo of the love we show.
In this world, a holy place,
Where seeds of grace and hope can grow.

## **Resonance of the Spirit**

In silence deep, the Spirit calls,
Whispers wrapped within the walls.
A gentle breeze, a soft embrace,
In every heart, the sacred space.

In every tear, a lesson learned,
For every bridge, a fire burned.
The light within, forever shines,
A sacred dance in holy signs.

With each new day, the hope revived,
In faith, our souls are kept alive.
The echoes of the past resound,
In every prayer, our peace is found.

Above the storm, the heavens gleam,
In darkest night, we still can dream.
Embracing love, we rise anew,
Together bound, me and you.

The Spirit's song, it leads the way,
In every night, it guides our day.
Through valleys low and mountains high,
In harmony, we soar and fly.

## **Litanies of Our Journey**

We gather here, our voices raised,
In litany of love, we're praised.
Step by step, on paths unknown,
In every heart, a seed is sown.

A journey marked by faith and grace,
In trials faced, we find our place.
Through shadows cast, and light we seek,
In every story, hope we speak.

With every prayer, our spirits lift,
The gift of grace, our hearts' sweet gift.
Together bound, through thick and thin,
In unity, our souls begin.

We walk as one, through storms we face,
In every challenge, we embrace.
The road is long, yet we are near,
In every sigh, the love is clear.

As litanies of life unfold,
In every word, our truth is told.
With open hearts and open hands,
We journey forth, where love commands.

## The Divine Cadence

In rhythm soft, the heart does beat,
A sacred dance, divinely sweet.
The world, a stage, where souls arise,
In every glance, the Spirit's ties.

Each moment flows, a river wide,
In every choice, we must abide.
The music plays, both loud and calm,
In discord found, we seek the balm.

With open ears, we catch the sound,
In quietude, our souls are found.
The cadence brings a promise near,
In silent faith, we cast out fear.

As life unfolds, the notes align,
In harmony, our spirits shine.
Each step defined, a sacred chance,
In every breath, the Spirit's dance.

The divine rhythm, it leads the way,
In every night and every day.
Go forth, embrace the love that grows,
In every heart, the cadence flows.

## **Threads of Light Through Time**

In ancient days, a tapestry,
Threads of light, weaved mysteriously.
Time intertwines, each moment we share,
In every soul, the love laid bare.

Through ages past, and futures bright,
Guided by faith, we walk in light.
Every heartbeat, a thread of grace,
In every life, the sacred trace.

From dawn to dusk, the colors blend,
In every path, the Spirit's lend.
A journey vast, through joy and strife,
In woven tales, we stitch our life.

As seasons change, the fibers weave,
In every memory, we believe.
Together strong, in love we climb,
Embracing faith through threads of time.

In every thread, a story spun,
In unity, we're never done.
For through our hearts, the light will shine,
In every soul, the love divine.

## Cosmic Reflections of Love

In the vast silence of night,
Stars whisper prayers of light.
Each twinkle a sacred embrace,
Guiding souls through empty space.

Boundless love in cosmic sea,
Embracing all that's meant to be.
Galaxies dance, a divine play,
In the heart's ethereal sway.

The moon casts shadows of dreams,
In her glow, hope softly beams.
Hearts aligned, pulse in sync,
In every breath, a silent link.

From stardust into this form,
We journey through love's endless storm.
In unity, we find our grace,
A tapestry of time and space.

Each moment, a glimmer divine,
Every heartbeat, a gentle sign.
Together we rise, hand in hand,
In love's embrace, forever we stand.

## Veils of Faith

In the quiet of morning light,
We seek truth beyond our sight.
Veils of faith wrapped around,
In stillness, the sacred is found.

Each prayer a whispering breeze,
Carrying hopes with gentle ease.
In shadows, belief takes flight,
Guided by the dawn's first light.

Mountains echo ancient chants,
In nature's embrace, the spirit plants.
The heart opens, surrendering wide,
In the depths, our souls reside.

Through trials, a pathway unfolds,
In our hands, the warmth it holds.
Together we rise, from ashes we bloom,
In the garden of faith, love finds room.

With every breath, we weave the thread,
Binding the living and the dead.
In veils of mystery, we walk free,
In faith, we find our eternity.

**The Sacred Mirror**

In the mirror of sacred sight,
Reflections dance in a soft light.
Each face tells a timeless tale,
Of love, of loss, and the veil.

Glimmers of grace in every glance,
In the stillness, we find our chance.
To see beyond the eyes that gaze,
Into the depths of love's warm blaze.

The sacred truth we hold so dear,
Awakens in the quiet here.
In each heartbeat, a divine spark,
Illuminating spaces dark.

With every tear that softly falls,
Wisdom echoes through the walls.
The mirror speaks of all we are,
A reflection of the guiding star.

In unity, our spirits align,
A tapestry where love will shine.
Through the sacred mirror, we see,
The beauty of our shared destiny.

## **Blessings of the Ancestral Winds**

Through the whispers of the trees,
Ancestral winds carry our pleas.
In their breath, a story flows,
Of our roots and where love grows.

Each gust a gentle embrace,
Binding us to sacred space.
Echoes of those who came before,
Guide us to an open door.

In the rustling leaves, a song,
Of connection where we belong.
With every step, we honor the past,
In the winds of change, we hold fast.

From the mountains to the stream,
We weave together our shared dream.
In the blessings of the air,
We find the strength to dare.

With gratitude, we walk the line,
Of generations, a sacred design.
In every breath, we feel their grace,
In the blessings of these ancient winds, we embrace.

## Testaments of the Heart

In shadows cast by faith's embrace,
Hope's light shines bright upon our face.
With love as guide, we find our way,
Each moment dawns a brand new day.

In trials faced, our spirits rise,
With prayerful whispers to the skies.
The heart holds secrets, pure and true,
In kindness shown, our strength renews.

Through every storm, we seek the peace,
In unity, our fears release.
Forgiveness flows like rivers wide,
In faith's embrace, our hearts abide.

The sacred texts our guiding star,
Illuminates both near and far.
With every breath, we lift our song,
In harmony, we all belong.

Thus, in this life, may we partake,
Of love entwined, never forsake.
The testament within our soul,
In unity, we are made whole.

## The Ripple of Prayer

A whisper carried on the breeze,
In stillness found beneath the trees.
Each prayer a pebble on the shore,
   Sending ripples forevermore.

With bowed heads, we seek to find,
The quiet peace that calms the mind.
In sacred moments, hearts align,
   In faith united, we entwine.

The rippling waters of the soul,
In every prayer, we feel made whole.
With each petition, hope expands,
A tapestry woven by gentle hands.

In midnight's hour, the heart's refrain,
   Echoes softly, our shared pain.
Through darkness light, it finds its way,
   In every prayer, we turn to stay.

Thus, let us gather, hand in hand,
   In gratitude, together stand.
For in the ripples, we shall see,
The boundless love that flows from thee.

## **Oracles of the Past**

Whispers of wisdom from days gone by,
Teach us patience, the reasons why.
In tales of old, the truth unfolds,
Each story woven, life extols.

The echoes linger in quiet space,
Reminding hearts of love and grace.
Through trials faced by those before,
We learn to stand, to seek, to soar.

In sacred texts, the oracles lie,
Guiding our spirits, teaching to fly.
With every lesson, a chance to grow,
In shadows of time, our seeds we sow.

With love as compass, we find our way,
In gratitude, we kneel and pray.
The voices of those who walked before,
Inspire us to unlock each door.

Thus, let us honor the paths they've paved,
With open hearts, their courage braved.
For in their stories, we find our fate,
Oracles guiding, both kind and straight.

## **Laments of the Wandering**

In footsteps lost upon the sand,
The wanderer's heart seeks a guiding hand.
Through valleys low and mountains high,
In every sigh, a silent cry.

The road is long, uncertainty waits,
With heavy burdens, we cross the gates.
Through trials faced and lessons learned,
The flame of hope within us burned.

In shadows cast by doubt and fear,
The soul's lament becomes sincere.
Yet through the night, a light we chase,
In every heart, we find our place.

Amongst the stars, our dreams take flight,
In every dawn, we seek the light.
With every journey, a story unfolds,
The lamenting heart in faith be bold.

Thus let us wander, hand in hand,
Together we rise, together we stand.
The path may twist, but love shall steer,
In laments found, our hearts draw near.

## Prayers in the Cosmos

In the vastness of the night,
Stars whisper secrets to the soul.
Heaven's light, a guiding fire,
Embraces us in its gentle role.

Each heartbeat sings a prayer,
Echoing through the cosmic sea.
Hands lifted, we seek the grace,
Of love eternal, wild and free.

Galaxies dance, a sacred waltz,
In the silence, sacred truths unfold.
Unity binds us, heart and mind,
In this tapestry, bright and bold.

Voices rise like incense smoke,
Carried on the winds of time.
Our hopes entwined with the heavens,
In harmony, we seek to rhyme.

As we pray beneath the stars,
May our spirits soar and gleam.
In the cosmos, we find our place,
Together, weaving every dream.

## **A Tapestry of Souls**

Threads of life, intertwined,
In the loom of sacred grace.
Each spirit, a vibrant hue,
Coloring time and space.

From mountains high to oceans deep,
Voices echo in the night.
In our hearts, a shared intent,
To spread love's eternal light.

The dance of moments, boldly spun,
In the hands of fate and will.
Together we weave our stories,
In the silence, hearts instill.

Every joy and every tear,
Stitches in this sacred cloth.
Bound by faith, through laughter shared,
Our souls embrace, no one is lost.

With each breath, we share our dreams,
In unity, our spirits soar.
In this tapestry of souls,
We are one, forevermore.

## **The Soul's Eternal Dialogue**

Whispers rise in twilight's glow,
Echoes of a heartfelt prayer.
In stillness, we seek to know,
The voice of love is everywhere.

Silent moments hold the truth,
In the depths of the heart's embrace.
A gentle nudge, a spark of light,
Guides us through this sacred space.

Questions linger in the dark,
Seeking answers, soft and clear.
The soul speaks softly to the mind,
In communion, drawing near.

In the dance of life and fate,
Every heartbeat tells a tale.
Each spirit's journey, a dialogue,
In whispers, like the evening gale.

Together we share this quest,
In the spirit's eternal flight.
In seeking, we find the peace,
Of love that shines through day and night.

## **Murmurs of a Shared Blessing**

In the hush of dawn's first light,
Soft murmurs speak of grace profound.
A blessing shared on every street,
In every heart, a love unbound.

With each step, we weave our hopes,
In kindness, our spirits intertwine.
Together we lift each other high,
In this journey, divine design.

The gentle touch of hands that care,
A radiant spark in human form.
In every smile, a glimpse of peace,
A warmth that breaks through the storm.

As the world breathes in and out,
May our intentions rise like songs.
In the harmony of giving hearts,
We find where each of us belongs.

So let us gather, heart to heart,
In moments filled with sharing light.
Murmurs of a shared blessing,
Illuminate the darkest night.

## The Voice of Time's Call

In whispers soft, the ages speak,
The ticking clock, a truth we seek.
Moments fleeting, yet so divine,
Each breath a gift, the sacred sign.

The past and future merge as one,
In the dawn, our journey's begun.
Hearts awaken to the chime,
In the stillness, we hear time's rhyme.

Echoes linger, a prayerful sound,
In every heartbeat, grace is found.
As shadows dance and lights unfold,
The story of us, forever told.

Every second holds a sacred spark,
Guiding souls through the deep and dark.
Embrace the now, release the chains,
In the essence of love, all remains.

## **Reverberations of Grace**

In the stillness, whispers of peace,
The heart's yearning finds its release.
Grace flows gently like a stream,
Softening earth in love's warm beam.

Hands uplifted, a prayer of light,
In the shadows, we seek the bright.
Miracles woven in each embrace,
Threads of hope in grace interlace.

Voices join in a timeless song,
Where the weary and lost belong.
In each tear, a glimmer of gold,
In every silence, a story told.

Grace reverberates, a soothing balm,
In the chaos, it brings us calm.
With every pulse, love's heartbeat shows,
In reverence, each spirit grows.

# **Reflections in Sacred Silence**

In sacred silence, truth reveals,
The heart's deep longing gently heals.
Still waters reflect the soul's own face,
In quiet moments, we find our place.

The universe breathes, a tranquil song,
In the void, we discover where we belong.
Eternal echoes touch the mind,
In silent prayer, our spirits aligned.

Time suspends in the peaceful wait,
In hushed breaths, we contemplate fate.
Every heartbeat, a note divine,
A melody woven in the grand design.

The soul awakens, a gentle stir,
In stillness, we find connection's blur.
A dance of light within the dark,
In silence, we ignite the spark.

## **The Spirit's Murmur**

In the quiet, a spirit calls,
Whispers echo through sacred halls.
Gently guiding with unseen hand,
In every heart, a promised land.

The murmur sings of love untold,
A tapestry woven from threads of gold.
Each breath carries a deeper tale,
In unity's embrace, we will not fail.

Softly spoken, the truth unfolds,
In shadows deep, the light beholds.
Awareness blooms in the still of night,
In the spirit's murmur, we find our light.

To walk this path in faith and grace,
Is to know the heart, to feel its place.
The journey whispers, ever near,
In the spirit's murmur, we shed our fear.

## Reveries of Our Journey

In the solitude of night, we seek,
Whispers of the stars, the tranquil peak.
Guided by light, our hearts align,
Together we walk, your hand in mine.

Paths unknown, yet faith our guide,
Through valleys low and hillsides wide.
In every step, a promise made,
In shadows deep, our fears will fade.

With each dawn, new grace unfolds,
Stories of love, forever told.
In prayers spoken, our spirits soar,
Holding the truth of what's in store.

As rivers flow and mountains rise,
We find our peace beneath the skies.
In silent echoes, the soul's refrain,
United we stand, through joy and pain.

At journey's end, we'll look back with pride,
For in this life, Your love's our tide.
In reveries sweet, our souls will blend,
A sacred bond that will never end.

## The Cadence of Kindred Spirits

In harmony, our hearts entwined,
A melody shared, the divine aligned.
Voices rise in a gentle prayer,
In this moment, we find You there.

Together we breathe, the sacred air,
In laughter and tears, all burdens share.
With every glance, a story told,
In the warmth of love, our spirits bold.

Kindred souls, on a path we tread,
With faith as our compass, we are led.
Through trials faced and triumphs won,
In every heartbeat, the journey begun.

As seasons change and rivers flow,
In the light of grace, our spirits glow.
Boundless joy is what we seek,
In every kindness, a light so meek.

So let us dance in the sacred light,
With grateful hearts, through day and night.
In communion true, with spirits wide,
Together, forever, by Your side.

## Faint Traces of Grace

In the stillness of dawn's soft glow,
We find the signs of love bestowed.
Faint traces linger in the air,
A gentle reminder that You are there.

With every step upon this earth,
We witness the miracle of birth.
In whispered winds, in rustling leaves,
The sacred speaks to those who believe.

A crumbled path, though worn and old,
Holds stories of warmth and love untold.
In the quiet moments, we find our way,
By grace's touch, in every prayer.

Through trials faced and burdens shared,
In our hearts' embrace, we know You cared.
With trembling hands and spirits free,
We gather strength from the mystery.

In every shadow, a light will gleam,
In the depths of night, we find the dream.
Faint traces guide us on the quest,
In the arms of love, we find our rest.

## Signs of the Sacred

In the rising sun, a promise shines,
In every heartbeat, Your love defines.
We gather 'round, in awe and peace,
In signs of the sacred, our fears release.

From the mountain tops, to the rolling seas,
Your spirit flows in the gentle breeze.
In laughter shared and tears that fall,
In every moment, we hear Your call.

In ancient woods where the wild things roam,
In the beauty found, we feel at home.
Our hearts ablaze in the light divine,
In nature's grace, our lives intertwine.

As stars align in the velvet night,
We seek the truth, in the silent light.
With open hearts, toward love we steer,
In every sign, we draw You near.

We honor the path that leads us home,
In all our journeys, we're never alone.
In sacred signs, our spirits grow,
Together we thrive, in love's warm glow.

## Journeys Through the Infinite

In the stillness of the night,
We wander paths unseen,
Guided by a silver light,
In dreams where we have been.

Each step a holy prayer,
Every breath a sacred song,
Through the cosmos we declare,
In love, we all belong.

The stars weave tales of old,
Whispers from realms divine,
Stories of the brave and bold,
Eternally entwined.

With each horizon drawn,
We seek what lies ahead,
For in dawn's gentle yawn,
Faith is ever fed.

So take my hand in trust,
Together we will soar,
Through the infinite's dust,
To find forever more.

## The Sacred Symphony

Amidst the quiet glow,
A melody takes flight,
In hearts where spirits flow,
A gift of purest light.

With chords of love resound,
In harmony we blend,
Each note a holy ground,
Where broken paths can mend.

Voices rise in unity,
An orchestra divine,
We dance in reverie,
Each step a holy sign.

The rhythms of the soul,
Reveal what hearts can share,
In music made whole,
We find our spirits rare.

So let the symphony,
Awake the sleeping night,
In sacred jubilee,
We rise to meet the light.

## **Treasures of the Spirit Realm**

In the depths of the heart,
Lie treasures yet to find,
Glimmers of a sacred art,
A journey intertwined.

Through valleys rich and deep,
We seek the precious gold,
In silence, wisdom speaks,
What never shall grow old.

As the sun begins to rise,
Illuminating grace,
In shadows, hope shines bright,
Awakening the space.

Each fragment holds a truth,
Stories of days gone by,
In the laughter of our youth,
A spirit dances high.

So cherish every gem,
With love etched in your soul,
For treasures never stem,
From a heart that is whole.

## **The Distant Bell's Toll**

In the twilight's soft embrace,
The distant bell does sound,
Echoes of a sacred place,
Calling all around.

With each chime, a prayer sent,
A longing for the peace,
In the heart where love is lent,
Find the soul's release.

Across the hills it sways,
In winds that gently call,
In rhythm with our days,
A bond that unites all.

So gather close your dreams,
As night enfolds the sky,
For in the softest beams,
Hope never says goodbye.

Let the bell's sweet toll guide,
Through shadows, take your flight,
In the stillness, abide,
Awakening to light.

## **Whispers of the Divine**

In the stillness, voices call,
Gentle murmurs, piercing all.
Guiding spirits, softly near,
Heaven's wisdom, pure and clear.

Clouds part ways to share the light,
Angelic glow, dispelling night.
Every heartbeat sings of grace,
In this sacred, hallowed space.

Should doubts arise within the soul,
Trust the whispers, make you whole.
Hidden truths in silence speak,
In this moment, hearts shall seek.

Nature's echo, prayerful sound,
In the forest, peace is found.
Winds that carry ancient songs,
In their embrace, the lost belong.

Kneeling low, in humble prayer,
Seeking presence everywhere.
Weaving faith, each thread aligned,
In the fabric, love defined.

# **Reflections of the Sacred Heart**

In the mirror of the soul,
Glistening dreams, making whole.
Hearts aflame with fervent desire,
Igniting faith, a holy fire.

Wounds of love, a gentle ache,
Boundless mercy, none forsake.
Holding close, compassion's gift,
In the heart, the spirits lift.

Through the trials, hope endures,
In the silence, love assures.
Every tear, a prayer released,
In the heart, all strife has ceased.

Radiant joy, resplendent light,
Guiding souls through darkest night.
In communion, hearts entwine,
Reflections of the sacred divine.

Beneath the stars, we gather near,
Whispered sorrows, shed our fear.
United in this bond we share,
In the heart, forever care.

## **Sacred Reverberations**

Echoes of a timeless grace,
Stirring deep, a warm embrace.
In the rhythm, spirits dance,
Caught in holy, sweet romance.

Chants of old in forests wide,
Ancient wisdom as our guide.
In the echoes, life takes flight,
Resonating through the night.

In the valleys, rivers flow,
Cleansing all, the heart must know.
Charms of nature, peace bestowed,
In their melody, we're bestowed.

Mountains rise with sacred might,
Touching heavens, kissing light.
Every heartbeat strong and sure,
In this love, we find the pure.

Lifting prayers to skies above,
In quietude, we find love.
Sacred songs, our spirits soar,
In reverberations, we restore.

## **Chants of the Lost**

In the shadows, voices weep,
Chants of those in sorrow deep.
Yearning for a guiding star,
In the night, they're never far.

Lost and wandering, hearts in strife,
Seeking solace, searching life.
In the echoes of their cries,
Hope arises, never dies.

Through the valleys, whispers cling,
Healing songs their spirits bring.
Every note a sacred plea,
In the darkness, we are free.

With each chant, the hearts unite,
In the fragments, love ignites.
Together through the storm they stand,
Hand in hand, a sacred band.

As dawn approaches, sorrows fade,
In the light, the shadows trade.
Chants of hope, a bright new day,
In the lost, the found will stay.

## Unity in the Divine Chorus

In the silence, we gather in prayer,
Voices risen, hearts laid bare.
Together we sing, a harmonious plea,
Echoing love that sets us free.

Hands intertwined, we form one chain,
Through joy and sorrow, through loss and gain.
Each soul a note in the sacred song,
In unity's arms, we all belong.

Ethereal whispers guide our way,
In the light of love, we choose to stay.
Bound by the truth that cannot sever,
Together we rise, now and forever.

From the depths of faith, we draw the might,
To face the dark, to embrace the light.
In every heartbeat, in every breath,
Unity's promise defies all death.

Together we wander, through trials we roam,
In each other's arms, we find our home.
With every act, the world we heal,
In the Divine chorus, our spirits feel.

# Reminders of the Hallowed Bond

In the stillness of twilight's embrace,
We remember love's sacred grace.
With every heartbeat, an echo rings,
A reminder of what communion brings.

Through trials faced, through joy anew,
We walk together, me and you.
Each moment shared, a thread in the weave,
In the tapestry of faith, we believe.

Sculpted by hands of the Divine above,
We are the vessels of endless love.
Connected by purpose, our paths entwine,
In the realm of the sacred, our hearts align.

The stars bear witness to our ascent,
In unity's bond, our souls are lent.
Each tear that falls, a prayer set free,
An affirmation of what we can be.

As the dawn breaks, new light does cast,
We cherish the memories, hold fast.
Grateful for moments, both near and far,
In the hallowed bond, we recognize the star.

## Reveries in the Light

In the morning glow, we rise and lift,
With hearts alight, we pray and gift.
Each ray that touches ignites our flame,
In reverence pure, we call His name.

Whispers of faith dance in the air,
Guiding our steps, a celestial care.
Every dream nurtured in holy grace,
In the Light's embrace, we find our place.

Beneath the heavens, together we stand,
In the sacred bond, hand in hand.
From shadows cast, we emerge as one,
Reveries whisper: we will overcome.

In every moment, a chance to shine,
To spread the joy, to intertwine.
With hearts attuned to the Divine call,
In reveries bright, we shall not fall.

Together we journey, through valleys low,
Carried by faith, we continue to grow.
In the Light we trust, our spirits soar,
In reverent dreams, now and evermore.

## **Communion of Forgotten Dreams**

In the silence, our voices blend,
A communion of dreams that never end.
In the darkness, hope takes flight,
Whispers of love in the soft moonlight.

Memories linger, like stars they gleam,
In sacred spaces, we share our dream.
Threads of connection, woven so tight,
In the fabric of heart, we find our light.

For every tear that journeys through,
The dawn will rise, and the world feels new.
In dreams forgotten, we seek the way,
To kindle the night, and embrace the day.

Through trials embraced, our spirits renew,
In the tapestry of life, we find the true.
Each moment a prayer, each thought a plea,
In the sweetness of communion, we shall be free.

Hallowed in grace, the dreams come alive,
United we flourish, together we thrive.
In the whispers of love, we cannot fail,
A communion eternal, our sacred trail.

## **Threads of Celestial Love**

In the quiet night, stars gleam bright,
Heaven whispers softly, holding tight.
Each thread we weave, a bond divine,
Stitched by grace, in love we shine.

Through valleys deep, on mountains high,
Faith guides our hearts, and lifts us nigh.
In every heartbeat, in every breath,
Threads of love conquer even death.

With open arms, we seek the light,
Together as one, we rise in flight.
Beyond the darkness, hope shall save,
In sacred love, we find the brave.

Let kindness flow, as rivers run,
In unity, we are never undone.
An eternal bond, in prayer we stand,
Embracing each other, hand in hand.

From whispers soft to thunderous song,
In the dance of life, we all belong.
Threads of celestial love intertwine,
In the heart of God, our souls align.

## Memories of Light

In dawn's soft glow, a promise made,
Memories of light in shadows fade.
Each moment treasured, a sacred sign,
In the tapestry of life, divine.

With every heartbeat, echoes flow,
Carrying whispers of what we know.
In the stillness, peace takes flight,
Guiding us back to the source of light.

Through trials faced, we learn to trust,
In love's embrace, all pain turns to dust.
A lantern shines, bright through the night,
Memories of light, forever ignite.

Each laugh and tear, a mark on time,
A rhythm of joy, a sacred rhyme.
In the garden, where blossoms grow,
Memories tend what the heart does sow.

As seasons change, we hold on tight,
In God's great love, we find our might.
Together we rise, our spirits bright,
In the warmth of the sun, we find our light.

## The Hymn of Our Souls

In the cradle of dawn, our spirits sing,
A hymn of love, to the Creator, we bring.
Each note a whisper, each chorus a thrill,
In harmony, hearts, the Divine we feel.

Through trials we bear, our voices unite,
In every struggle, we find our sight.
With penitent hearts, we lift our song,
In the grace of faith, we all belong.

From valleys low to the heavens above,
We cherish the gift of unending love.
In sacred silence, our souls take flight,
Illuminated paths, glowing so bright.

Together we walk on this journey long,
In the arms of hope, we courageously throng.
With each gentle breeze, a prayer we send,
The hymn of our souls will never end.

With gratitude deep, we stand in grace,
In the light of truth, we find our place.
A melody woven in the heart's embrace,
The hymn of our souls, forever in space.

## Resonance of Belief

In the heartbeats of prayer, we find our strength,
Resonance of belief spans the length.
Through the echoes of time, faith stays clear,
In unity, we conquer each fear.

With every sunrise, hope paints the sky,
In the canvas of life, we learn to fly.
In whispers of love, we hear His voice,
The spirit ignites, we rejoice in choice.

With hands lifted high, we seek the true,
In the garden of grace, we are renewed.
Each step a journey, each road a guide,
Resonance of belief walks by our side.

In the face of doubt, we stand as one,
Together in faith, the battles are won.
Our hearts intertwined, a sacred weave,
In the warmth of love, we shall believe.

With the strength of the ages, we rise and sing,
The resonance of belief shall always bring,
A light in the darkness, a beacon bright,
Together in faith, we soar in the light.

## **Glimpses of Transcendence**

In silent prayers, the soul does soar,
Seeking the light on a distant shore.
Whispers of grace in the shadowed night,
Carrying hope on the wings of light.

Stars that gleam with a holy fire,
Guiding the heart to its deep desire.
In every moment, divinity speaks,
In the stillness, the spirit seeks.

Mountains high, valleys below,
Nature reveals what we long to know.
Every creature, a sacred sign,
In the tapestry, the love divine.

Through trials faced and burdens borne,
In darkest hours, the soul is reborn.
With faith as a lantern, we journey on,
Towards the dawn of a new day's song.

In every heartbeat, the truth resides,
In the midst of chaos, the calm abides.
Beyond the veil, we catch a glimpse,
Of the eternal, where love outprints.

## The Cannon of Creeds

In paths untrodden, we find our way,
With ancient words that guide the day.
From sacred texts, the wisdom flows,
In every chapter, our spirit grows.

Rituals born from a fervent heart,
In unity, we play our part.
Echoes of faith in the silent night,
Together we rise, shining so bright.

Beneath the steeple, our voices blend,
In harmony, our souls descend.
With hands uplifted, prayers ascend,
A testament to love that won't bend.

In every creed lies a sacred seed,
Nurtured with love, fulfilling the need.
Across the ages, the truth remains,
In every heartbeat, religion gains.

Through trials and doubts, we stand as one,
In the arms of grace, our fears are done.
Beneath the heavens, we pledge our faith,
In the light of love, we find our place.

## Morpheus' Embrace

In dream-like whispers, the spirit drifts,
Through veils of slumber, the soul uplifts.
In shadows soft where silence sighs,
Awakened visions, the heart complies.

In gentle folds of Morpheus' care,
We find the truth in the stillness rare.
Beneath the stars, our worries cease,
In sacred dreams, we discover peace.

As twilight falls, the mind takes flight,
Through realms of wonder, into the night.
Every heartbeat, a sacred drum,
In the silence, the spirits come.

Through whispered prayers, the night unfolds,
In tender tales, the heart consoles.
With every dream, a promise made,
In Morpheus' arms, we are unafraid.

Awake, aware, to the world anew,
With love and faith, our spirits grew.
In the dance of dawn, a new day calls,
Through Morpheus' embrace, the light enthralls.

## Chronicles of the Faithful

In the tapestry woven, stories arise,
Chronicles penned in the darkened skies.
With every heartbeat, a tale we share,
Faith in our souls, beyond compare.

Pilgrims we are on this sacred quest,
Seeking the truth, we know no rest.
In struggles faced and joy embraced,
In every trial, with love we're graced.

The light shines brighter, in shadows cast,
Through every moment, from first to last.
With hands held high, we journey forth,
In kindness found, we acknowledge worth.

Together we gather, a circle complete,
In faith united, our spirits meet.
In every story, a truth unfolds,
In the hearts of the faithful, a love that holds.

At journey's end, when shadows fade,
In unity, we will not evade.
Through chronicles rich, we sing our song,
In the embrace of love, we all belong.

## Voices from the Beyond

In whispers soft, they share their light,
Guiding souls through darkest night.
A melody of love, pure and deep,
Awakens hope within our sleep.

Each prayer a bridge to realms unseen,
Where faith resides, serene, pristine.
In sacred tones, they call our name,
Reminding us we're all the same.

Through trials faced and burdens bore,
Their wisdom echoes evermore.
With every tear and every smile,
They walk beside us mile by mile.

In moments still, the heart can hear,
The silent hymn that calms our fear.
Embrace these whispers, hold them near,
Their love unfailing, always near.

So let us rise, uplifted skies,
With voices joined, our spirits fly.
Together as one, we find our song,
In hope and grace, where we belong.

## **Celestial Remnants**

Starlight drapes the weary earth,
A gentle glow of sacred birth.
Each twinkle tells of ancient grace,
A story shared in the vast space.

In shadows cast by fleeting time,
Echoes linger of the divine.
Through every dawn, their light persists,
A reminder of the holy tryst.

Celestial bodies in their dance,
Invite us to this sacred chance.
To gaze above and find our course,
In the universe, we're not forced.

A tapestry of spirit sewn,
In threads of glory, brightly grown.
Each moment woven, intertwined,
In love, the essence of mankind.

With every breath, feel sacred sparks,
Guiding us through the autumn parks.
For in our hearts, remnants reside,
Of celestial love, our eternal guide.

## Threads of Faith Intertwined

Woven patterns, soft and bright,
Binding hearts in shared delight.
Threads of faith, so deeply sewn,
In every moment, love is shown.

From every trial, strength we gain,
Each tear a part of joyful pain.
A tapestry of lives aligned,
In grace and mercy, we are blind.

Together we rise, together we stand,
With faith as our anchor, hand in hand.
Through every storm, our spirits soar,
In unity, we find our core.

As visions dance in vibrant hues,
We seek the path that speaks the truth.
In whispered prayers, a sweet refrain,
Echoing softly, love will remain.

So let us walk, with purpose clear,
In every challenge, call them near.
For threads of faith, they intertwine,
Creating a bond, divine design.

## The Echoing Silence

In the silence, spirits stir,
Bearing witness, hearts confer.
In quietude, we search for light,
Finding strength in the still of night.

A sacred hush, the world held fast,
In echoes of the souls that passed.
Through whispers soft, their essence guides,
In the void where love abides.

With every breath, we feel them near,
In silent moments, they appear.
A gentle touch, a knowing glance,
In silence, life begins to dance.

Through trials faced and hopes reborn,
In the stillness, we are sworn.
To seek and find, to listen close,
In echoes, love becomes our host.

For in this realm of void and grace,
Silent prayers find their place.
The echoing silence speaks the truth,
In hearts awakened, eternal youth.

## Revered Moments Suspended

In silence, hearts entwined, we pray,
A moment held, like dawn's first ray.
With every breath, we seek the light,
In reverence, we find our sight.

In shadows deep, the spirit stirs,
A voice that calls, yet softly purrs.
Each whispered hope, a sacred song,
In unity, we all belong.

Through trials faced, our faith aligns,
In storms of doubt, the love defines.
The path once lost, now bright and clear,
In every tear, the truth draws near.

The sacred ground beneath our toes,
Where gentle winds of grace do blows.
Together we rise, in humble awe,
Embracing all that life will draw.

As stars above begin to shine,
We gather strength, our hearts divine.
In every moment, hand in hand,
We stand as one, a faithful band.

## Faith's Lasting Echo

Through valleys low and mountains high,
In quiet hearts, the thoughts comply.
Each echo carries hopes anew,
In faith's embrace, we find what's true.

The whispered prayers that touch the sky,
In every tear, the spirits fly.
A journey vast, with grace we tread,
In sacred trust, our souls are fed.

When darkness looms and shadows creep,
We hold our faith, its promises keep.
Through trials faced, our spirits blend,
In every struggle, love will mend.

In moments fleeting, find the peace,
With every prayer, our worries cease.
For in the stillness, souls unite,
In love's vast echo, pure and bright.

Together, as the days unfold,
Our hearts reflect the truth retold.
In every step, in every breath,
Faith's lasting echo conquers death.

## Whispers of Old

In ancient tomes, the secrets lie,
With each turn, the spirits sigh.
The wisdom flows like rivers wide,
In whispered tales, we confide.

The candle flickers, shadows play,
In quiet corners, echoes stay.
From ages past, the voices rise,
To guide us through life's lows and highs.

In humble places, grace appears,
A soothing balm for troubled fears.
Through prayers spoke, our hearts align,
In unity, we seek the divine.

With every heart, a story shared,
In brokenness, we learn to care.
Through whispers of old, our spirits soar,
In ancient truths, we crave for more.

Unfolding like the morning sun,
Together we rise, we'll not outrun.
For in the quiet, wisdom glows,
In sacred bonds, the love bestows.

## The Spirit's Embrace

When daylight fades, the night unfolds,
In every heart, the warmth upholds.
The spirit dances, free and bold,
In every breath, a story told.

Among the stars, a guiding light,
It leads us through the dark of night.
Each glimmer speaks of love unseen,
In every moment, pure and clean.

In tender grace, we find our peace,
Through trials faced, our burdens cease.
The spirit whispers, soft and low,
In gentle strength, it helps us grow.

Together bound by faith we lift,
Each humble heart, a precious gift.
Through love's own arms, we brave the space,
In every soul, the spirit's grace.

As dawn arrives, we hold it near,
In every heartbeat, we persevere.
For in this life, we dare to chase,
The endless love of spirit's embrace.

## **Divine Remembrances**

In the quiet of dawn, we rise,
Whispered prayers reach the skies.
Hearts open wide to His grace,
In each moment, His love we trace.

With every breath, we find peace,
From burdens heavy, we seek release.
Guided by faith, we walk the way,
In His light, we live and pray.

Amidst the storms, His voice we hear,
Promises kept, we hold so dear.
Through trials faced, we grow strong,
In unity, we sing His song.

The stars above, a cosmic sign,
With every heartbeat, His love divine.
In communion, our spirits align,
With open hearts, His truths we shine.

Let us gather, hand in hand,
In His mercy, we take a stand.
With gratitude, we praise His name,
In each life, His love the same.

## The Testament of Togetherness

In sacred circles, we unite,
Bound by love, we seek the light.
With open hands, we share our fears,
In laughter sweet, we dry our tears.

With every word that we proclaim,
We write together, our hearts aflame.
A tapestry of faith and grace,
In every smile, His warm embrace.

Through trials faced, our spirits soar,
In unity, we seek to explore.
Hand in hand, we walk this road,
In every burden, our love is showed.

The echoes of hope fill the air,
In each gesture, we show we care.
With faith as our anchor, we rise,
In every heart, His light implies.

Together we stand, steadfast and true,
In love's embrace, we start anew.
For in our bonds, His spirit shines,
In every moment, our faith entwines.

## Revelations in Stillness

In silent moments, wisdom calls,
In hush of night, the spirit sprawls.
Each quiet breath, a sacred pause,
In stillness deep, we see His cause.

The murmurs of nature sing His praise,
In twilight's glow, our hearts ablaze.
With every heartbeat, a truth unfolds,
In gentle whispers, His love foretold.

Beneath the stars, in cosmic grace,
In every silence, we find our place.
As shadows dance, His light commands,
In tranquil waves, peace gently lands.

In solitude, the soul takes flight,
In every shadow, we find His light.
With open hearts, we listen near,
In stillness deep, His voice is clear.

Each fleeting moment, a chance to see,
In every heartbeat, His mystery.
For in the quiet, love's reveal,
In sacred stillness, we learn to heal.

## Harmonies of the Soul

With every note, our spirits sing,
In perfect harmony, His love we bring.
Through rain and shine, our hearts entwine,
In joyful rhythms, His grace we find.

In every challenge, we rise anew,
With faith as our guide, we journey through.
In the melody of life, we sway,
In every challenge, love lights the way.

The music of creation flows,
In every heartbeat, His presence glows.
In unity, our voices blend,
In every note, His truths transcend.

With gratitude, we lift our praise,
In sacred circles, our hearts ablaze.
Each song a testament, each chord a prayer,
In the symphony of life, His love we share.

Through trials faced, our souls unite,
In the dance of faith, we find our light.
For in His harmonies, we are whole,
In every echo, we discover our soul.

## Sacred Footprints

In silence, paths of grace do lie,
Step softly where the angels sigh.
With every stride, a prayer unfolds,
In sacred whispers, love retold.

The earth beneath, a canvas pure,
Where holy echoes find their cure.
We walk in faith, with hearts aflame,
Each footprint bears the Father's name.

Beneath the stars, our hopes aligned,
Each soul entwined, all humankind.
Together we rise, in truth we stand,
With sacred footprints in this land.

The journey weaves through light and shade,
In every moment, the divine made.
Let kindness guide each step we take,
In the heart of love, our bonds awake.

So let us tread this path so wide,
With faith as our eternal guide.
In every stride, let spirits soar,
In sacred footprints, forevermore.

## **Voices Beyond the Veil**

In whispers soft, the spirits call,
From realms beyond, where shadows fall.
Their echoes linger, light as air,
A symphony of love and prayer.

Through time and space, their wisdom flows,
Guiding hearts where the river grows.
In silence deep, we hear their song,
Uniting all, where we belong.

Among the stars, their laughter rings,
A tapestry of holy things.
In dreams they tread, with gentle grace,
Inviting us to seek their face.

Let not fear cloak the night so clear,
For in their presence, love draws near.
Beyond the veil, they shine so bright,
In every shadow, reveals the light.

So listen well, and keep the flame,
For voices brave still call our name.
In unity, their truth we find,
Connecting souls, both near and blind.

## Celestial Echoings

In skies so vast, the stars align,
Each twinkle, a note divine.
A cosmic dance, where spirits play,
In celestial echoings, night and day.

The heavens sing with voices grand,
As love's refrain sweeps through the land.
In every rhythm, a heartbeat heard,
In sacred harmony, we are stirred.

Through ancient tales, the truths arise,
Painting wisdom across the skies.
In every breath, a prayer takes flight,
In celestial echoings, pure delight.

Let whispers guide us to the throne,
Where grace abounds, we're not alone.
In every longing, a hope ignites,
With celestial echoings, we reach new heights.

So raise your voice, let praises soar,
In unity, we seek much more.
With open hearts, our spirits sing,
In celestial echoings, love takes wing.

## The Call to Unity

In the stillness, a voice does cry,
"Come together, let love draw nigh."
Beneath the sky, all spirits meet,
In the call to unity, our hearts beat.

With hands extended, we stand as one,
Under the warmth of the rising sun.
Each breath a promise, each smile a bridge,
In the call to unity, we honor our pledge.

From every corner, a story shared,
In diversity's beauty, we find we're bared.
Together we rise, through joy and pain,
In the call to unity, our strength remains.

Let kindness pave the paths we walk,
In every word, let love unlock.
For in the gathering, the spirit thrives,
In the call to unity, our hope alive.

So heed the call, let the circle grow,
In unity's embrace, let the love flow.
With open hearts, we find our way,
In the call to unity, we shall not sway.

## Divine Mosaics

In the tapestry of grace, we find,
Colors woven, love aligned.
Each thread a story, each hue a prayer,
Seeking the light, forever to share.

Wonders manifest in skies above,
Patterns reveal the Creator's love.
In quiet whispers, the heart composes,
A symphony of life, where faith supposes.

Lives intertwine like branches of trees,
Beneath the sheltering, gentle breeze.
In every heartbeat, a sacred song,
Echoing truths where we all belong.

The artist's hand, in every creation,
Fills our souls with divine elation.
With every step, we learn to see,
The mosaic of life, our unity.

Glory encircles the humble and meek,
In their simplicity, love's voice speaks.
Together we stand, a radiant whole,
In the divine mosaic, we find our role.

# **Heartstrings of the Cosmos**

A symphony plays beneath the stars,
In every dial of fate, we are ours.
Strings vibrate softly, resonating with grace,
Binding our spirits in time and space.

Each heartbeat echoes, a celestial sound,
In the quiet moments, peace is found.
From galaxies vast to the smallest bloom,
We dance to the rhythm, dispelling the gloom.

Threads of existence, we weave in delight,
In the fabric of time, love ignites.
With every breath, we connect and unite,
In the cosmos' embrace, forever in light.

The universe whispers, its secrets unfold,
Every star shines bright, a tale to be told.
In the depths of our hearts, the truth sings clear,
Drawing us closer, erasing all fear.

Together we journey, hand in hand,
On this path of love, eternally planned.
In the heartstrings we share, a bond ever strong,
In the dance of the cosmos, we all belong.

## **The Unseen Connection**

In silent chambers, where souls collide,
A force unspoken, where love abides.
Threads invisible, binding us tight,
In the depths of darkness, we find the light.

Each gentle touch reveals a soul's truth,
In the dance of ages, the wisdom of youth.
Forever entwined, in paths we roam,
In this unseen bond, we find our home.

Mirrors of spirit reflect our grace,
In the wandering hearts, we embrace.
With open arms, we share our plight,
In the unseen connection, we hold on tight.

The echoes of laughter, the sighs of peace,
In every encounter, our hearts find release.
Though apart we may be, in spirit we meet,
In this sacred journey, we are complete.

Through trials endured, we learn to see,
In the fabric of love, we're meant to be.
The unseen connection, a treasure so rare,
In the dance of existence, we find our prayer.

## Shadows of the Beloved

In the twilight whispers, shadows play,
Echoing memories of yesterday.
The beloved's warmth, a soft embrace,
Surrounds our hearts, a sacred space.

In every tear, a story flowed,
Paths of longing, love's heavy load.
Yet in the darkness, hope shines bright,
Guiding our souls toward the light.

Shadows reveal what the heart can't speak,
In the silence of yearning, we find the peak.
With every heartbeat, we rise and fall,
In the presence of love, we answer the call.

Beneath the stars, where dreams unite,
We share our burdens, take flight in the night.
In the shadows, the beloved appears,
Whispering truths as we conquer our fears.

Hand in hand, through valleys we tread,
In the shadows of love, we're never misled.
For every shadow simply reflects,
The light of the beloved, our hearts connect.

Milton Keynes UK
Ingram Content Group UK Ltd.
UKHW021857151124
451262UK00014B/1323